ONLINE DATING'S TRADE-SECRET : learn these easy techniques to succeed in online dating.

Marvin V. Morris

Table of contents

Introduction

Before one delves into the complexities of online dating, there are many things that one must understand about it. It is not all fun and games. Although it may seem like the easiest thing in the world, online dating is not straightforward. It has to be taken seriously, else, things can go out of hand. Every game has its own rules, and if you don't know them all, you'll never improve as a player or ultimately come out on top. You may learn the guidelines for playing online games and how to win by reading this book.

Chapter1
Tastes Vary

There are so many different types of individuals around. Just take a glance at you. How many individuals do you recognize?

Sizes, builds, forms, and characteristics all vary greatly.

And that just deals with outward appearances. And the plot completely changes when it comes to the characters. Return to your former classes and have a peek around as you go down memory lane.

One setting where we have the opportunity to connect closely with many different individuals is a classroom. We get to interact with a variety of individuals from quite varied backgrounds and get to know them personally. So how many of your peers did you get along with?

Not as classmates, but as humans, is what I mean. Was it simple to get along with everyone? Because of this, we often have best friends or clichés in our classes.

We don't have to like everyone and we don't have to. While one person's likes and interests may be completely at odds with ours, another person's tastes and interests may coincide with ours.

Therefore, the dating experience is mostly the same. However, there are conditions in place here. Unlike in a classroom setting, most individuals go on dates to find a life partner, which is a more remarkable goal. Before two individuals decide to spend the rest of their lives together, 101 things need to be compatible.

Many individuals believe that they can handle dating on their own. They could be correct since no one is more familiar with a person's preferences than they are.

Perhaps the majority of us can choose without assistance, but wouldn't it be beneficial to learn a few tips on dating in general, especially online dating? This article was created with this goal in mind, so that the thousands of people who are now using online dating services may get the most from them.

What Differs Online Dating So Much?

We, as humans, have been on this planet for tens of thousands of years. People have been selecting mates since before humankind began. People pick their life partners in a wide variety of ways since cultures throughout the globe are so diverse.

But compared to the history of humanity as a whole, the idea of finding a life mate with the aid of the Internet is a relatively new one. The Internet and computers have greatly impacted man's life, therefore it is not surprising that the Internet has become a factor in choosing a compatible spouse as well.

Simply described, online dating is the process of meeting a spouse online via a machine, specifically a computer. Hundreds of content individuals from all over the world have found compatible spouses through internet dating, which makes the concept and the procedure new.

To be honest with you, though, a lot of unfortunate people have been duped and abandoned by the same procedure. So let's go into the specifics of online dating to ensure that you get a spot on the first list.

Chapter2

The Magic of the Internet

Online dating is no different from the Internet in that regard. Because of the seemingly limitless communication options provided by the Internet, online dating has found this characteristic to be both a blessing and a curse.

Before the encounter, people may start again and learn all there is to know about one another. Tastes and preferences, likes and dislikes, hobbies, and obsessions may be shared privately so that the two parties are not at all strangers when they encounter occurs. Amazing, isn't it?

However, this potential for limitless communication also opens up a lot of room for deceit. The capacity to utilize, abuse, and misuse the same object is a magnificent gift bestowed to the human species. Naturally, online dating has also been and continues to be utilized for despicable ends.

It could be a practical joker or someone with more sinister motives looking to prey on some unsuspecting victims who are abusing this facility. This is the reason why doing a little bit of homework is a smart idea before leaving.

You do not, however, need to worry since the hard work has already been done for you. All you need to do is run your eyes over the lines below, and you will be ready to strike it rich.

Chapter3

How Did Online Dating Become So Popular?

The cause is rather obvious. The same factors that made the Internet so well-liked also explain this phenomenon. A whole new world of interaction and communication is made possible via the Internet. And the following are the explanations behind this.

Speed

Imagine what used to occur in the past when people had to rely on reliable mail service. A person back then had to wait one or two days for a letter to reach someone who resided in the same state as them. It would take the second person one or two days to answer, and one or two days would pass before the first person received this letter.

Therefore, a single letter would last for a whole week. But things have changed completely since then. Amazingly, the first letter and answer were completed in only two minutes!

E-mail brings two individuals together more quickly than waiting, which may make the heart grow fonder.

Privacy

Additionally, the Internet offers complete privacy. In the complete privacy of one's bedroom, bathroom, or any other location of one's choice, one may communicate with another person. Thanks to chat and e-mail features, there is no need to worry about being overheard or eavesdropped on (yuck!).
Opportunities and Options

The one thing that the Internet lacks is actual contact, but it does provide other choices like voice chat and video conferencing. But who would want to initiate physical contact immediately early in a relationship?

Is there a better method to start a date where you can see the individual, speak to them, and hear their voice?

Economy

The Internet has made all of this and more possible, and the greatest part is that it costs you almost nothing. You just need a PC, and who doesn't have one? and access to the internet (how could anybody survive without one? and you are ready to go. The only thing you could want is a step-by-step manual on how to select your ideal date, and you can get it right here!

So why are we still waiting?

Be Specific With Your Goals

Man is, as we all know, a social creature. But the human being is also a lonely one. (And by "guy," we also mean women.) Man craves companionship.

Not just from friends and family, but also from that particular someone with whom he or she can share those sweet nothings, those everyday joys, and sorrows, someone with whom they may start a whole new life together and raise their own family.

Finding a life partner is now a basic necessity for man. And dating is the most often utilized technique for this. Please keep in mind that when we speak about dating in the truest meaning of the term, it is not to be considered a step toward sleeping together. Much more than that is involved. It is the first stage in selecting a life companion, and internet dating has now greatly streamlined the procedure.

Chapter4

Marriage Versus A Casual Relationship

Your actions and desires are fully up to you at this point. To avoid coming off as nosy, I'd want to clearly distinguish between the types of dating that are involved in these two missions.

Of course, we are all adults, so let's conduct ourselves accordingly. We want to have fun in a casual relationship. Remember that fun may mean many different things. Therefore, in this case, the person who is the target of one's desire is not interested in a committed relationship.

If both partners have the same opinion, everything is OK since they fully comprehend one another and have low expectations for the relationship. There is no place for grief with this.

The issues arise when one person is focused on something important while the other is purely trivial. Therefore, you should be extremely clear about what you are seeking right from the start and be very upfront about your objectives with the other person.

You should also be certain of the other person's intentions at the same time. Just keep in mind that there should be mutual knowledge, if not of the relationship itself, then at least of its nature.

Of course, there is yet another scenario in which a casual connection might develop into a more committed one. Yet again, under such circumstances, it is your instincts that may guide you in differentiating between good and negative things.

Anybody may be played for a fool or taken for granted, regardless of strength. Being abandoned is never a pleasant feeling. For the love of God, be cautious if you want to start a casual relationship! We shall discuss marriage later since it is a very other matter.

Dating Is Born Out of a Basic Need

Let's face it, although sex unquestionably plays a significant role in dating, it is by no means the main driver.

Important! Sex may be on everyone's mind in the carefree youth when fresh hormones are being pushed in and out. However, when one grows (remember, this does not imply becoming older and grayer), sex recedes into the background while mutual support, preferences, teamwork, caring, and sharing take center stage. When we start to imagine creating our universe, we need a partner—not simply someone to sleep with—to share it with.

Every person has a basic urge for sex. We all possess the capacity to both provide and receive sexual pleasure. But after giving it some thought, you realize that this want is the outcome of another urge.

Every person has a more fundamental want to reproduce and have children, and it is this urge that gives birth to such strong sexual desire. However, dating is the most respectable way to sate any craving.

No one, not one of us, is whole without a mate, and many dates to satiate this desire. As a result, the remainder of this guidebook will focus on finding the ideal life mate rather than the ideal sex partner.

Online dating will remain popular.

Let's face it: dating couldn't possibly get much better. The actual thing about dating is online. Think of the previous system of evening balls or other social events as a comparison. Imagine that you are among a large group of men and women seeking compatible companions.

Let's say you run across one or two individuals

with whom you click right away. The moon will be the only thing keeping an eye on you as you lead this individual outside onto a balcony.

You get to converse with this individual for hours on end, without interruption. You get to talk about likes and dislikes, and when it's time to go, you pledge to meet the next day in a location that you both find pleasurable. Days and weeks pass during these conversations until you ultimately realize that this is THE person you want to spend the rest of your life with.

Eventually, you meet in more public settings, hold hands, and even kiss. You start eating lunch and supper out and becoming closer as a couple. It's time to say "I do" when the timing is appropriate and you have made your choice.

Sigh! Doesn't that seem like a charming fairy tale?

Well, it's unnecessary. Because the idea of internet dating is exactly what has been mentioned above, it may be your love tale. We have proof that everything might go well for you if you click the proper buttons. You can see for yourself how popular online dating has already become by looking at the statistics provided below.

One of the nicest aspects of internet dating, as I've

already indicated, is how much anonymity it offers. You can talk on the phone for hours, have video conferences, or do whatever else you choose without catching anybody else's notice or drawing the wrong sort of attention. Everything becomes as discrete as it can be with only a computer and Internet connectivity. But may I also add that in addition to that, we also need a little bit of common sense, otherwise we can end up in the grasp of one of the many horrifying creatures that are out there.

Another benefit of online dating is that it allows you to save a lot of money that you would otherwise have to spend every time you went on a date. Numerous individuals consider online dating to be a fantastic convenience for these and many more personal reasons, which are the main drivers of its popularity

Chapter5

How To Get The Most Out Of Online Dating

Many individuals who decide to attempt internet dating often wind up with burned fingers and hair.

Online dating is more complicated than it seems, which is why we decided to compile this guide. To get the most out of it, you must understand how to approach the situation. The majority of individuals don't enjoy taking risks, and they especially don't want to take any chances while looking for a life mate.

However, you may rest easy knowing that we'll cover all the dos and don'ts in this booklet, making the whole procedure simple and pleasurable for you. You will find detailed advice on how to start online dating in this guidebook.
Since we are confident in our readers' capacity for making judgment calls, we don't plan to provide many pieces of advice on the subject. Our goal is to simply provide a few pointers that we think will be helpful to our readers as they continue their search for the ideal spouse.

Getting Going

Where angels fear to tread, only fools enter.

Before you go outside and begin dealing cards, you need to have a strategy. Be confident in who you are and what you desire. We are not required to behave in the same way just because anybody and everyone is free to write anything they want in a chat room.

The fact that everybody may access the Internet is a fantastic feature. However, this same characteristic draws individuals of different backgrounds to it. But it doesn't imply that everyone in a chat room is like that just because a lot of individuals that join there have nothing but trash on their thoughts. You may receive the proper answer if you keep your composure and cling to your sense of class.

The Internet is full of good people, but it all relies on what you do. The golden rule here is to treat people as you would want to be treated. The game has no set rules. There are gamers everywhere. But you don't have to be a ruffian just because some people around you are.

The only thing that will get you the answer you desire is your strategy.

I don't believe it makes much sense to decide on the spur of the moment that you want to utilize the internet to find a date. Simply declaring "I'm

available" in a chat room is the equivalent of putting oneself up for sale and is unlikely to get the desired results.
Everyone has to recognize that everyone in a chat room is on an equal footing. Contrary to popular belief, you shouldn't dress up and join a chat room as you would a ballroom. The most eligible individual (read that as the sexiest member of the opposite sex) then gets your attention and moves in your direction while everyone turns to gaze at you.

Only in James Bond movies do things like that occur, and we all know that Bond never enters into a committed relationship. It’s all fun and games for him.

How Do You Begin?

The first piece of advice we'd like to provide you is to DELAY entering a singles chat room in search of a potential date. We are all aware that the majority of these chat rooms are almost overrun with individuals that simply have sex on their minds. Therefore, no matter what you ask for, it always comes to that, defeating the objective. You'll never meet someone who somewhat shares your hobbies and preferences.

It may get pretty frustrating at times. Starting well

is the goal. The subject suddenly shifts to the three-letter term while you and the other person are getting to know one another better. Then you sigh and have to decide whether to block their communications or run the risk of their disparaging you in a public chat room. Usually, you have to completely exit the chat area.

In other words, it is the simplest thing to convince someone to sleep with you but if you are seeking something more lasting, like a life companion, then you are going to have to be a bit more patient. Finding the best of the bunch is challenging. But when you do discover it, the effort will have been worthwhile.

Therefore, you may test the entire thing out from a new viewpoint rather than entering a singles' chat room. You could consider going backward.

Beyond Appearances

Try to think about the things that interest you and the things that you would find intriguing in a person while you sit for a minute or two.

By 'things' over here I am not talking to bodily features. I'm not talking about anything that could catch your attention about someone's looks. Again,

the line between a serious relationship and a casual connection has to be defined. Physical characteristics are usually important in casual relationships. We are more interested in a person's physical appearance and natural abilities.
The physical attributes, however, are less significant if we are in a committed relationship. In this case, compatibility is perhaps the most crucial aspect. Additionally, there are several attributes that we will undoubtedly be on the lookout for. We are discussing mental faculties.

Although it may seem weird, this notion is real. The premise is that one may learn to enjoy someone's appearance over time. You will begin to like someone if you find their character to be acceptable. Even if someone does not have the appearance of a movie star, it is still possible to fall in love with them. One of the tricks nature pulls is that.

Before formally committing to a relationship, many individuals insist on seeing the other person's image. They may have their reasons, of course, but I believe that a choice like this, which is mostly focused on appearance, is more suited for a casual relationship. After some time, it will inevitably lose steam. After all, how long can you maintain eye contact with someone? What happens if the other person doesn't return your gaze?

What if you discover the individual glancing at someone else? Would it be worse? If you are considering a serious relationship, looks may be important, but they are by no means the most important thing and should never be used as the deciding factor.

Similar Interests

The other side of a human being cannot be seen through a piece of glass, as it is impossible. A person is more like a diamond, which when held up to light reflects and deflects light such that a variety of hues are seen. We are intricate.

We all have a wide range of interests, thus there is no need that them to coincide. Fortunately, there are fewer hobbies than there are people. Thus, we will undoubtedly come across many others who share our interests. And if we can locate someone who fits that description, then our quest should be over. What kind of things interest you? You need to learn more about it.

However, you may need to give it some serious thought before you scale down your preferences. There may be several activities you like doing but haven't given much consideration to.

Sports or outdoor pursuits may be among your hobbies. Alternatively, you might consider hobbies like social work, crossword puzzles, or religion. Please note that the words I've listed here are merely suggestions; keep the conversation going.

You may have very different preferences and interests. So leave them alone. And once you've determined what your interests are, you've accomplished half the work.

What About People Catch Your Eye?

Probably the most significant portion of the narrative is this. We must all take a seat and consider what traits we would value in a partner. Even though you have similar hobbies, you could not get along with someone.

For instance, just because you like talking a lot doesn't always imply that you would enjoy another person who does the same. There cannot be a conversation if two persons attempt to speak at the same time.

The same goes if the other person is likewise a quiet, reserved kind; in that case, there won't be any conversation at all! Here, the term is "compatibility." Partners' interests should be complementary rather than at odds.

Chapter6

Keyword Searches

After deciding what it is about someone that fascinates you as well as your hobbies and preferences, attempt such keyword searches on a search engine like Google.

Here, you're not supposed to promote the fact that you're looking for a life companion. No matter how nicely you phrase it, once you enter a singles chat room, it loses its nuance. So avoid doing it that way. You may recall that we discussed working backward; here is how it is carried out.

In a later chapter, we'll explain how to present oneself in the best possible light, but for now, let's speak about meeting Mr. or Mrs. Right. It's interesting to observe that choosing between two options or falling in love with someone is not difficult in this situation. Making the correct decision and falling in love with the right person is the challenging part.

Favorites vs. Dislikes

The second thing you may do is make a list of traits in people whom you detest. No, I'm not kidding. Likes and dislikes are just as essential, if not more so. We all have to sometimes make concessions, but if we start by tolerating behaviors that we detest, it will eventually harm the relationship.

I want to provide a word of warning in this area. When courting, a lot of individuals make mistakes. They put up their finest act, which is excellent, but they also attempt to be extremely flexible and accommodating, which is NOT excellent. They often overlook the fact that they will be spending the rest of their life with the person they are attempting to impress; they won't just be going on a camping vacation together.

It is thus important to avoid being too "oh so very accommodating and adapting."

You have the freedom to cling to your specific preferences. And forget about trying to change the offender's bad behaviors down the road if you had any such ideas.

The instant you begin attempting to change or persuade the person out of their habits, whatever they may be, the term "encouraging" changes to "nagging," and even if the person can break the habit, they will dislike you less for it.

Things don't operate that way. Therefore, it is better to be aware of the traits and behaviors that you detest in others and to avoid 'lesser mortals' that share such traits.

Your ability to choose wisely improves if you have a general understanding of your preferences. You don't need to worry or be very concerned that you may not find anybody at all, given the sheer number of individuals in the world. If you are doing what you are doing correctly, that is, barking up the appropriate tree, you will succeed in finding him or her.

Some individuals even think that everything is

predetermined. Who shall wed who has been predetermined, and ultimately, only what is predetermined will take place? I'm not sure about that, but I am aware that dating expedites the process.

Another option is to do nothing and let nature run its course. Oh, how wonderful nature is. The best thing we could do is to give nature a helping hand because choosing a partner involves a lot of chemistry.

First, friends

Try to view this endeavor as an effort to make a lot of friends, and I mean good friends, rather than as a search for a future husband or wife. Friends who make you laugh and with whom you can laugh out loud. Not everyone can make us laugh, and I don't just mean when a comic does it. Here, we're referring to pals.

Truly, having plenty of friends pays off. It enriches one's life. You can be who you are with friends, which is the finest part about them. They are also free to be themselves around you. Therefore, you must let everything out. We must always keep in mind that in addition to being a good husband or wife, a spouse should also be your best friend.

The majority of couples make this error. They often see their wives and friends as being in distinct categories. Although it's OK to have your pals, your spouse or partner should always be your greatest friend.

It should be someone you can confide in, who understands, who can give you a soft hug when things go wrong, and who can make even the darkest day more cheerful.

This is all a pretty long way from having sex, right? For this reason, we did state previously that choosing a life mate should be based on factors other than appearance and sex. The marriage proposal must follow a natural progression, and it should not be the first thing you say after becoming friends with someone. You can't just say, "Hey, you know what, I believe we have the same preferences, so let's get married," for example.

Of course, you may say that, but it wouldn't be very tasteful. What would you do then if you found out that the buddy you made and the one you were crossing your fingers for was already married?

Do you own a vehicle? The solution is thus straightforward—all you have to do is run over that person's spouse to get rid of the undesired component. Wrong! It just isn't done. You may continue to be friends with that individual while focusing on a different path. Who knows, you could even come across someone better. All you need to do is redealt your cards after shuffling them.
I believe you now understand what we meant by "working backward"? Good. There is still a catch to this procedure. One of the new acquaintances you met may have also read this book, in which case the proposal may come from the opposite side.

If it works, great; you don't have to do the rite.

Ms. Wrong and Mr. Right

But what if the person who proposes wasn't truly who you were looking for? Of course, you have a choice; you may accept it or reject it. However, there is something here to think about. Finding someone we love is great, but isn't it preferable to discover someone who also loves us?

But I also want to put something over here. What if someone does approach you and make a proposal, but you regrettably show no sign of interest? You have every right to decline the offer, but if you can, please do it politely. No need to bruise the ego of the other person. They are a buddy.

of yours, and I'm sure you love them dearly. However, if you are certain that you cannot be married to this person, declining their proposal is preferable to divorcing them.

In the gentlest manner possible, try to express your emotions.

Chapter7

Making Yourself Look Like A Million Dollars

Although nobody is flawless in this world,
we may still strive to look our best. Giving nature a helping hand is quite appropriate. Work on improving your profile, image, and physical attractiveness.

The maxim "This is me, whether you like it or not, it's your issue" is held by many individuals. I won't alter my behavior. No one is requesting that you alter, so what are you attempting to do? frighten folks away?

The truth is that words like those just serve to highlight your insecurities. Each of us struggles with insecurity to some extent, but some more than others. We come out as stern and indifferent when it comes to enhancing our looks because of this insecurity.

What are you so terrified of? I'll tip you off. Everyone has similar fears, no matter what they are. The majority of individuals in this world are neither for us nor against us. They are preoccupied with themselves.

Although it takes a lot of effort to present oneself well, curiously, this is the one area that individuals often overlook. When it comes to describing ourselves, the majority of us are relaxed. We need to work a lot harder on how we portray ourselves.

We would have liked to assist you in creating a profile of yourself that was as remarkable as possible if we had known you better personally. However, it is difficult to get to know every one of our readers personally.

You need not fear, however, since we have done extensive research in this area, and if you follow our recommendations, you will be able to create the profile of your dreams.

THE DREAM STYLE

It is impossible to put too much work into creating a profile. It is something that has to be taken very seriously. Please don't be careless with this matter. If you were applying for a job, wouldn't you spend a lot of time crafting the perfect resume?
Well, the majority of us work for an average of four to five years. How about a relationship? We most certainly do not get into a relationship with the hope that it would only continue for a few years.

We must realize that a relationship is worth far more than a career since it is likely the most significant choice you will ever make. So let's talk about how you may polish your profile today.

Of course, you can save time and effort by hiring a professional to complete the task for you. Of course, you may have to spend a little money, but it could be worthwhile. Many individuals are reluctant to include a photo on their profile. I don't want to pursue the matter, however. Although it helps make your profile appear nicer to include a photo, you are free to omit one owing to privacy concerns.

The best thing you could do is send your photo along as an attachment or a file after you feel comfortable conversing with someone and are certain that they do not have any nefarious motives. However, it's ideal to do this on the premise of reciprocal trade. If you were to know someone's appearance but the other person was kept in the dark, and vice versa, it would be unjust.

The Mirror's Image

Now that we are at the image, please, for the love of God, send over a nice picture if you are sending one of yourself. Please do not compromise on the quality and make sure it is current. Hire an expert to do the task for you; using modern digital methods, they may achieve extremely good results.

Before the picture is taken, work on your expression at the same time. Try out numerous faces while standing in front of your mirror until you find one that you believe suits you the best. Also, keep in mind that you must be smiling in the photo. The traditional hangdog look and the "butter-will-not-melt-in-my-mouth expression" are inappropriate. Smiling is free and it certainly brightens someone's face.

Chapter8

You are Unique

Consider that for a moment. Examine your image in the mirror. Do any of your acquaintances think you resemble them?
Although we all have the same exterior characteristics—one nose, one mouth, two eyes, and two ears—we all seem quite different.

So why do we have to sound similar while sharing the same structural components if we may look so different? Consider yourself in a different light. When developing your profile, don't simply think about your preferences; also think about your best traits. What exactly are endearing traits?

These are the characteristics that people enjoy about you. Of course, we seldom think about these things, but maybe we should. Asking your closest friends why they like you is what I would advise. Who knows, you could be surprised by their responses! However, you will at least have a better sense of what you can include in your profile.

The exercise below might be used to determine your personality type. I won't suggest that the outcomes are 100% foolproof, but they may be intriguing nevertheless.

Watch out for Immediate Intimacy

Many people think that e-mail will never be as warm or as personal as the traditional letters and cards that people used to send via the postal service. That may be the case, but email has the benefit of being present-tense.

There is a tendency for intimacy to develop even before you realize it because you are conscious that the person with whom you are conversing is reaching out to you in the same manner that you are reaching out to that person.

When someone pressures you for information that you must provide instantly, the medium no longer matters, and unless you are well-prepared, you can let some things slip out.

Four ways to identify a liar

We won't use single chat rooms designed exclusively for internet dating, as was previously suggested. Instead, we shall participate in niche chat groups. So asking someone really precise questions on the topic of interest would be a highly effective technique to determine whether they are lying. You shouldn't spend your time on someone if they stumble or make evasive responses.
Another option is to record whatever information the person decides to provide with you right away. Then,

when you see them again, casually inquire about the information you recorded the first time. If there is a discrepancy between the two data, you may be certain that the person is lying.

Ask the person questions that seem to be generic but should have a very clear goal, such as what the person is looking for in a relationship like this. Write down the response. Repeat the question after two or three meetings to see if the two responses agree.

You might try acting as if you've spoken with the person previously and jokingly asking whether they are such-and-such a person (make something up). You could also attempt complimenting the individual by saying something like, "I liked talking to you the other day. You were charming, etc. If someone is susceptible to such cheap flattery, it is obvious that they enjoy chatting with people while assuming different identities.

meeting in person

There is no justification to put off a face-to-face meeting once you have established a telephone connection because the relationship has already begun to take flight. So why are we still waiting? However, there is no need to rush things. You shouldn't seem too eager to meet this person, either.

Let the choice to meet develop over many phone conversations. And before you meet, there are several things you may keep in mind.

Chapter9

Offline Dating: How To Make That Great Impression

There are several factors in your favor when you date online. For instance, you do not need to worry about looks since the other person cannot see you. You may focus all of your efforts on sounding funny and knowledgeable.

However, there is a myriad of factors to pay attention to when you are sitting in front of a person. Many individuals have the opinion that maintaining looks is not very essential. They believe that being oneself is more important.

It has a passable sound. However, you must maintain your look, at least on your first date. You should make every effort to prevent such blunders since the other person shouldn't feel embarrassed to be seen out and about with you.

Let's begin by discussing your look. Even though I just said that you don't have to dress to kill, you must seem well-groomed. Pay close attention to your teeth, hair, and nails. Since having poor breath is the biggest turnoff, make sure to check it as well.

You shouldn't dress in a loud way that draws unwanted attention. Select clothing that fits you well while also making you feel comfortable. Ladies, please use caution while applying makeup and keep in mind that it should enhance rather than conceal your appearance. It is better to stay away from loud colors.

Of course, you should smell nice, but don't go overboard. We don't want the other person to remember you just for that one overwhelming fragrance. Men, please be careful to choose more manly odors, like musk, or scents from nature. Keep it as light and elegant as you can, ladies.

But for the joke to work, it must be spontaneous and appropriate for the circumstance. Avoid practicing jokes since they tend to seem, well, practiced.

Charm is the essential word here. Put all of your charms to good use. Make an effort to be as courteous and thoughtful as you can. Instead of taking over the discussion, encourage the other person to speak. Asking about the other person's employment might help you start a conversation since people often like talking about themselves. Show consideration for what the other person has to say.

What do you do if you see that the other person is monopolizing the discourse, then?

Gifts?

It is a good idea to bring a present since it makes a nice first impression, but keep in mind that while you are courting, your gifts should only be flowers or chocolates. Try to learn what the other person enjoys in terms of flowers and chocolates while you are conversing. Giving someone who is allergic to flowers is not a good idea.

The goal of your presentation should be to leave a positive and long-lasting impression rather than to win over the recipient. Spending a lot on a first date is pointless since there is no law stating that everything must go well the first time. Don't go overboard while maintaining a professional appearance.

However, if the other person forgets to bring you a present, make sure to quickly reassure them that everything will be OK. Keep the other person from feeling uncomfortable. That is a great way to lighten the discussion. The following time, you may humorously request that the other person bring you a present.

Here, I'm not referring to two-timing. Keeping your options open rather than placing all of your eggs in one basket, is what I'm trying to say. Don't rely only on one individual since you don't want to lose heart if it doesn't work out

www.ingramcontent.com/pod-product-compliance
Lightning Source LLC
LaVergne TN
LVHW020531160826
845677LV00015B/3995

* 9 7 9 8 8 4 8 3 4 1 6 8 3 *